Contents

Action Stations!

When I arrive at work I get dressed into my uniform for roll call. We're all given riding positions on the fire engine and told what our duties for the day will be. Suddenly we are interrupted by a shout! That's the firefighters' name for an emergency call. In our station an alarm bell rings loudly.

The Controller takes the call and the Watch Commander lets us know where we are going and what kind of emergency to expect. This time it is a house fire with a person possibly trapped inside. The fire engine pulls out of the station with its lights flashing and siren on – we're in a hurry!

The quickest way to the truck.

Let's go!

WHAT'S IT LIKE TO BE A..?

FIREFIGHTER

Elizabeth Dowen   Lisa Thompson

First published in the UK 2010 by
A & C Black Publishing Ltd
36 Soho Square
London
W1D 3QY
www.acblack.com

Copyright © 2009 Blake Publishing
Published 2009 by Blake Education Pty Ltd, Australia

ISBN: 978-1-4081-2872-5

A CIP catalogue record for this book is available from the British Library.
Written by Lisa Thompson and Elizabeth Dowen
Publisher: Katy Pike
Series Editor: Eve Tonelli
Designers: D Brown, Cliff Watt and Clifford Hayes
Printed and bound in China by Leo Paper Products.

Cover image © shutterstock

All inside images © Shutterstock and iStockphotos except p3 (tl), (tsl), (br),
p6 (b), p10 (tr), p11 (tr), p13 (b), p15 (mr), p18 (b), p25 (tl), (tr) – NSW Fire
Brigades; p29 (b), p31 (m) – Meeka Bailey; p31 (b) – Mark Holland; p33 (tl)
– Paul Dewick; p35 (b) – Arnold Genthe; p36 (b) – Kevin Kohlhagen.

With grateful thanks to the NSW Fire Brigades and the NSW Rural Fire
Service for their generous support and assistance.

This book is produced using paper made from wood grown in managed,
sustainable forests. It is natural, renewable and recyclable. The logging and
manufacturing processes conform to the environmental regulations of the
country of origin.

All the Internet addresses given in this book were correct at the time of
going to press. The author and publishers regret any inconvenience caused
if addresses have changed or sites have ceased to exist, but can accept no
responsibility for any such changes.

We drive to the fire quickly but safely. We see smoke billowing out from a house when we enter the street. As soon as the fire engine pulls up, we jump out to make a quick assessment of the situation whilst our driver gets the pumps started.

The emergency lights and siren let everyone know we're coming and to get out of the way!

Time to check for people trapped inside.

The Watch Commander calls the Controller to let him know we have arrived and to give our assessment of the scene. The Controller confirms that a police car and ambulance are only minutes away. My partner and I put on Breathing Apparatus, grab a hose line and enter the house.

Is there anybody in here?

It is black with smoke so it's virtually impossible to see anything. Heat and fire are building in the back room. We have to move fast.

5

My partner and I search the house for the missing person and find her near the back door. She is unconscious from the smoke. We drag her outside, away from the fire and into the care of ambulance personnel who are now on the scene.

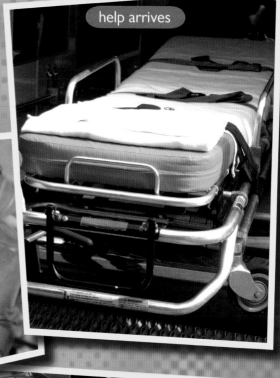

help arrives

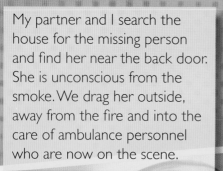

Rescuing people is our number one priority.

Firefighting Team Work

Firefighters always work in teams. The minimum team number is two. This partnering system helps firefighters to protect each other and to ensure the safety of all team members.

Working with partners helps keep everyone safe.

DIDYOUKNOW?

LONDON'S BURNING!

The Great Fire of London in 1666 destroyed almost 80% of the City of London – including over 13,000 houses and 87 churches. Amazingly, only about six people were actually killed.

The police have arrived and are blocking off the street as neighbouring houses are evacuated.

Streets may need to be closed off for public safety.

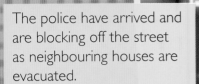

FIRE LINE DO NOT CROSS

We try to get the fire under control.

My partner and I drag the hoses around to the back of the house and start to fight the fire from the outside. Water shoots into the house and onto the flames and thick smoke that are pouring out the windows as the fire grows. We will have to work fast to get the fire under control and stop it spreading.

BEING A FIREFIGHTER

Being a firefighter is a combination of routine activities, intense training and life-threatening situations – and those activities switch instantly at the sound of an alarm.

7

How I became a firefighter

My dad was a retained firefighter, so I have been around fire crews and fire stations all my life. I took part in a full-time induction training programme for 16 weeks.

Community spirit is strong with rural firefighters.

The practical side of the firefighting training programme included:

- fire behaviour and firefighting

- basic rescue techniques and entering smoke-filled rooms

- fitting protective clothing and using breathing apparatus

- handling foam and other types of fire extinguishers

- using ladders, hoses, knots and other equipment

- first aid, and health and safety.

After this training I joined my fire station for a probationary period of two years.

Now my job is so varied! We provide lots of other emergency services, as well as firefighting. We deal with bomb alerts, and we rescue victims from accident sites like car crashes and other dangerous situations, such as flooding. Sometimes we are even called in to manage chemical spills (or other hazardous materials).

I also get involved in fire prevention work. This can include giving presentations to schools and other groups, and inspecting buildings to make sure they meet fire safety.

Firefighters don't just put out house fires.

On top of it all I have routine station duties, such as inspecting, cleaning and maintaining equipment, carrying out practice drills and taking part in training.

Next year I'd like to get my Large Goods Vehicle (LGV) licence, so I can drive the fire appliances.

Cleaning up after a road accident with hazardous materials involved.

Firefighters regularly attend practice drills, exercises, lectures and other forms of training.

Once qualified, you can work towards S/NVQ Level three in Emergency Fire Services. There are extra courses (S/NVQs) in the following roles: Crew Manager, Watch Manager, Station Manager, Group Manager and Area Manager. Gaining extra qualifications like these will help you to progress in this career.

Can you work in confined spaces like this?

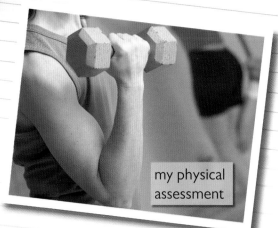

my physical assessment

What's it worth?

Starting pay for a firefighter is around £17,000, rising to £21,000 with experience. At the higher levels, assistant chief officers and chief officers/ firemasters are not paid on fixed scales, and salaries vary with different fire authorities. Retained firefighters are paid additional fees, in line with their rank.

Firefighter training

Firefighters are constantly trained and tested in the use of fire appliances, equipment (extension ladders, breathing apparatus, pumps), handling hazardous materials and fire science and behaviour.

This is how we can breathe inside burning buildings.

Qualities needed to be a good firefighter

- ★ mental alertness
- ★ self-discipline
- ★ courage
- ★ endurance and strength
- ★ mechanical aptitude
- ★ ability to work as part of a team
- ★ sense of public service
- ★ ability to handle heights, stress and confined spaces
- ★ ability to assess risk quickly
- ★ capability to handle trauma when working with accidents and emergencies

Firefighters have to stay fit!

It takes all levels of firefighters to make a great team.

We have to work together.

Firefighter ranks

The first step up the ladder is to the rank of **Leading Firefighter**, followed by **Sub Officer** then, after about five years in the service, to **Station Officer**.

On each fire engine there will be:
No.1 OIC (officer in charge)
No.2 Driver
No.3/4 BA (breathing apparatus) wearers
No. 5 BA Entry Control Officer

11

LIFE AT A FIRE STATION

Firefighters work on a roster system. When a firefighter is on night shift, they sleep at the station with the rest of the crew.

Firefighters normally work a 42-hour week, which can include shifts and overtime.

How does a roster work?

A four-day roster system means
- 2 × 10 hr days (8 am – 6 pm)
- 2 × 14 hr nights (6 pm – 8 am)
  - then four days off before the cycle starts again.

DIDYOUKNOW?

False alarms

Of all the emergency services, the fire brigade attends the most false alarms. Alarms are often set off by mistake or because they are not working properly.

ALL ALARMS HAVE TO BE RESPONDED TO – JUST IN CASE.

Checking equipment is vital to ensure safety.

Sunday

Day Shift

Time \ Day	
8am	BREAKFAST
9am	Station Duties – Clean station
10am	CHECK EQUIPMENT –Truck, generators, pumps, breathing apparatus, air tanks, gas detection units, rescue equipment.
11:30am	LUNCH
12:30pm	Continue checking equipment and repairs.
1:30 pm	UNIFORM CHECK
2pm	DRILL – Discuss gas detectors and new fire procedures from head office
3pm	The shout
4pm	Back at the station
6pm	Shift over – no fire today, thank goodness

16

3 pm The shout is given. This time it is not a drill, it's the real thing. Everyone puts on their personal protection equipment as quickly as they can and jumps into the fire engine. The details are sent through from the Controller to the Watch Commander. It contains information such as:

• nearest cross street to the fire

• map reference to get there

• type of fire, potential hazards and any other information known about the incident.

3:15 pm We arrive at the scene and see there is no fire. The call was set off by a faulty fire alarm. While we are there, we assess the scene for fire safety.

4 pm We return to the station. We recheck all the equipment and make sure everything is ready for the next call out. The Watch Commander writes an incident report.

6 pm The day shift is over, the night shift team arrives. It's time to go home.

DIDYOUKNOW?

As well as about 41,000 full-time firefighters in the UK, there are around 17,900 'retained' or part-time firefighters, mainly in rural areas and small towns. About 1,400 people work as volunteer firefighters in Scotland.

PROTECTIVE CLOTHING

Emergency work can be very stressful, physically demanding and often very uncomfortable. You may face hazardous conditions such as extremes of heat and cold, high or unstable locations, enclosed spaces, smoke-filled buildings, all weather conditions and working both in the day and at night. You can also be exposed to danger from buildings collapsing and vehicle fumes and explosions.

This gear helps us work right in amongst the flames.

- helmet with visor and neck flap
- flash hood
- gloves
- fire-resistant coat
- fire-resistant trousers
- special woollen socks
- chemical and fire-retardant boots

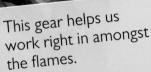

Who else is called to the scene?

Ambulance

Ambulance teams work closely with firefighters if there are people trapped or injured at the scene of an accident or fire. An ambulance team is made up of two officials.

Both officers are also paramedics. Paramedics are trained to treat patients involved in life and death emergencies and accidents. They give emergency care to patients at the scene and during the drive to hospital.

Police

If a fire may have been deliberately lit or people have been killed or injured, the police are informed at the same time as the fire service. At the scene, police officers will put up barriers to keep people away, interview witnesses and gather evidence.

Once the fire has been put out, the police arson squad will work with fire investigators to determine if the fire was deliberate. If it was started on purpose, it is their job to find the person or people responsible.

inside an ambulance

An ambulance is on the scene when urgent medical treatment is needed.

Paramedics look after us too!

The police will come too if there needs to be an investigation.

Fire Facts

Fire is fast

In less than 30 seconds, a small flame can get completely out of control and become a major fire. It takes only minutes for thick, black smoke to fill a house. Most fires happen in the home, when people are asleep.

Every second counts when a fire starts

If you wake up to a fire, it won't be long before the whole house is engulfed in flames. You won't have time to grab valuables. There is only time to escape. Just get down low and go, go, go!

Fire is deadly

Smoke and toxic gases kill more people than flames do. Fire uses up the oxygen you need to breathe and produces smoke and poisonous gases. Breathing in even small amounts of smoke and toxic gases will make you drowsy, confused and short of breath.

DIDYOUKNOW?

TOO FAST
Every 30 seconds, a house fire doubles in size.

9731-105 ST.

Fire is hot

Heat is a bigger threat than flames. Just the heat of a fire can kill.

Inhaling super-hot air scorches your lungs and melts your clothes to your skin. In five minutes, a room can become so hot that everything in it ignites at once. This is called a flashover.

Flashovers can cause temperatures to reach up to 1,100 degrees Celsius.

Fire is dark

Fire starts brightly, but quickly produces black smoke and complete darkness. If you're woken by a fire, you may be blinded, disorientated and unable to find your way around your home.

DIDYOUKNOW?

BACKDRAFTS

A backdraft is a roaring, explosive surge of fire that is produced when air is introduced to an oxygen starved room – usually by opening a door or a window. The gases still in the room from a smouldering fire then explode. Firefighters must watch out for areas with few openings that have been burning for some time and could cause backdrafts.

Back at the house fire

Eventually the fire is put out.

Once the fire is out, we enter the house with a fire investigator to look for the possible cause of the fire. It looks like this fire started in the clothes dryer. There is nothing suspicious about the fire so we do not need the police to be further involved.

ready to go again

F. 4303

checking the hose

FORESTVILLE

051

After the fire investigator has finished gathering evidence for his report, we begin our clean-up. When we get back to the station, all the equipment we used will be cleaned (or replaced) and checked so the fire engine and the equipment is ready for the next shout.

Fire Stats

- In the UK, Fire and Rescue Services attended 722,000 fire and false alarm incidents in 2008/09.

- The number of fires in the UK fell by 9% in 2008/2009 to 128,000.

- In Scotland, people are twice as likely to die in house fires as people anywhere else in the UK.

- 90 people die each year because the battery in their smoke alarm was flat or missing.

- Over half of home fires are caused by cooking accidents.

- More than five fires a day are started by candles.

- Every three days someone dies from a fire caused by a cigarette.

- Faulty electrics (appliances, wiring and overloaded sockets) cause around 7,000 house fires across the country every year.

LPG
Highly flammable

Possible sources of fires

DIDYOUKNOW? **CAR FIRES**

Every year in the UK, over 100,000 cars (about 300 a day) go up in flames and around 100 people die as a result. 65% of these fires are started deliberately to cover criminal activity, to make a fraudulent insurance claim or as an act of vandalism. One in 12 reported stolen cars will be burnt out. Many other vehicle fires break out simply due to a lack of basic maintenance and can be prevented.

flaming research

Space flames

Flames change in space. They turn into tiny, glowing, floating balls. Floating flame balls were first discovered in 1984 when a researcher at NASA's Lewis Research Centre was performing an experiment in the Microgravity Drop Tower. The scientist noticed that in the tower, simulating weightless space conditions, the flames broke apart into tiny balls that floated around the experiment container.

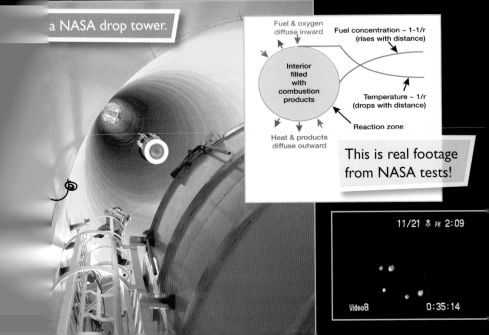

a NASA drop tower.

Fuel & oxygen
diffuse inward

Fuel concentration ~ 1-1/r
(rises with distance)

Interior
filled
with
combustion
products

Temperature ~ 1/r
(drops with distance)

Reaction zone

Heat & products
diffuse outward

This is real footage from NASA tests!

11/21 木 PM 2:09

Video8   0:35:14

Flame balls are different from the flames we see on earth. They are dimmer and produce much less heat.

Some flame balls flew around in a spiral pattern like these DNA strands.

Flame balls could hold the key to reducing how much fuel we use.

Astronauts then conducted flame ball studies on the space shuttle. The astronauts named the flame balls to help them keep track of the strange things they saw them doing. Flames named Crick and Watson flew around in a spiral pattern like DNA. Howard was a very strange flame that headed for the outer walls of the experiment chamber and quickly went out.

One of the biggest flame balls was called Zeldovich, after the Russian physicist who predicted flame balls in 1944. But it was a flame named Kelly that lasted the longest. Kelly burned for 81 minutes and became the longest-lasting flame ball ever recorded.

Researchers hope to learn more about fire and combustion from flame ball experiments to help us better understand fire back here on earth. Flame ball research could help create better engines for cars and planes that run on far less fuel – just like flame balls which require little fuel to keep burning.

FIRE SPECIALISTS

Some firefighters train to become experts in specialist fields.

Within this area of origin, the investigator looks for what may have started the fire, known as the ignition source. Firstly, they identify all the potential ignition sources. Then, by analysing test results, they rule out the sources one by one, until they find the fire's most probable source.

Fire investigators

Fire investigation is a specialist branch of forensic science. Fire investigators determine the origins and causes of fires. They work with the police arson squad – they collect evidence, interview witnesses and prepare reports on fires in cases where the cause may be arson or criminal negligence.

These specialists work out what happened.

A fire investigator carefully observes and interprets the smoke, heat and fire effects to track down the place where the fire started. This is known as the area of origin.

This is how a house looks after a fire.

Forensic fire specialists

A forensic fire specialist is someone who is trained in how fire works and behaves. Forensic fire specialists may work for the police arson squad or be employed by insurance companies, law firms or businesses for specialist investigations.

For example, if it is assumed that a hair dryer is the ignition source, the forensic fire specialist must determine that the hair dryer really did cause the fire and be able to explain how the hair dryer malfunctioned to cause the fire and why.

The real CSI

Forensic refers to something that is discussed in court. Therefore, forensic experts are people who present evidence in court relating to their special field of study.

This is fire detective work!

Cracker, the fire investigation dog

Greater Manchester Fire investigation Team includes a canine member, Cracker. Cracker is highly-trained to sniff out accelerants which may have been used to start a fire.

an airport-based fire crew

Fire safety officers

Many companies train members of staff to become fire safety officers. As well as training in fire safety procedures, fire safety officers, like firefighters, undergo continual hazmat (hazardous material) training.

Hazardous materials require specific handling and disposal procedures. This is because they are highly flammable or toxic and pose a potential threat to people and the environment.

Specialist firefighting teams

Some companies and industries have their own specialist firefighting teams. Most major airports have their own firefighting teams who have particular expertise in battling fires involving highly flammable materials such as kerosene-based jet fuel. They are trained in using equipment designed specifically for fighting aircraft fires and are also trained in aircraft passenger rescue.

Dangerous materials need to be handled with care.

This could be a danger to your health.

an airport-based fire appliance

Fire education

Part of our job is also to educate the public about fire safety and make sure people understand the work that we do.

A firefighter giving out information to the public.

Flood rescue

Firefighters can be involved in flood rescue. Some fire services have specialist teams of swift water and flood rescue technicians and boat operators. A Fire Service National Flood Support Centre can be set up to coordinate specialist responses in major floods.

Deliberate Fires

Nearly 10% of all fires are believed to have been started by children. Therefore, it is very important for firefighters to teach parents and children about the real dangers of playing with fire. We promote sensible behaviour around fire to reduce the terrible cost to people and property.

DID YOU KNOW?

EXPLOSIVE STUFF

In 15 minutes, a firestorm can give out as much energy as a nuclear explosion!

Firefighters Worldwide

Across the world, firefighters have different hazards to contend with. In recent years large forest and scrub fires have been a real problem in California, Greece, and France. In Australia they call these fires bushfires. Often volunteer firefighters are trained to support rural fire brigades.

The Australian bushfires

The times of greatest bushfire danger are when there is a combination of extreme weather conditions (dry, hot, windy weather) and a build-up over several years of dry twigs and leaves. Long droughts in forested areas, that dry out vegetation and dry up moisture in the soil and the water reserves in dams, make the landscape fire sensitive.

When the weather patterns bring strong, hot, dry winds and the temperature rises, the conditions are set for a dangerous bushfire season.

Firestorms

A firestorm is a blaze which is so intense that it creates its own wind system. It is most commonly a natural phenomenon, created during some of the largest bushfires, forest fires, and wildfires. The Great Peshtigo Fire and the Ash Wednesday fires are two examples of a firestorm. Firestorms can also be deliberate effects of targeted explosives such as occurred as a result of the aerial bombings of Dresden, Hamburg, Stalingrad, Tokyo, the atomic bombing of Hiroshima and Nagasaki and The Blitz during World War II.

DRY THAT HAY!

Hay can self-combust. If it gets stored while it is too wet, it gets so hot it catches alight on its own.

Hot and dry weather is the worst time for bushfires.

Types of bushfires

Ground fires – burn slowly in logs and tree roots, usually long after the main fire has passed.

What is a firebreak?

A firebreak is a line of land that has been cleared of plants, trees and leaf litter. It looks like a narrow track. Firefighters burn off these tracks to limit a fire's access to fuel.

ground fire

Surface fires – are the most common type of fire involving the burning of grass, scrub and bushland.

Dry conditions can mean bushfire danger.

surface fire

Crown fires – occur when the bushfire is very intense. Rising heat, from burning leaves and bushes on the ground, sets the treetops alight and the wind drives the fire forward through the upper canopy of the forest.

Bushfire factors

  lack of rain
+ low humidity
+ dry vegetation
+ wind
+ high temperatures over
  long periods
= bushfire danger

crown fire

27

The Global Fire Monitoring Center (GFMC) is based in Germany. It is designed as a information and monitoring facility, for all national and international agencies involved fire and other disaster management. It monitors the world's fires by satellite.

Each country has agencies monitoring fire risks, especially in hot and dry climates where the risks of large fires are greatest.

For example, the Bureau of Meteorology in Australia calculates the maximum fire danger for each day. This helps fire authorities predict the speed at which the fire will spread and the difficulty of keeping it under control.

On days of 'High' to 'Extreme' danger, fire authorities may declare a total fire ban and put firefighters on stand-by in case of a fire outbreak.

Bushfire danger levels		
Light green		low
Light blue		moderate
Yellow		high
Orange		very high
Red		extreme

The Al 'Alziziyah Desert

Satellites provide information on fires.

DIDYOUKNOW?

HOTTEST PLACE ON EARTH

Al 'Alziziyah in Libya recorded a temperature of 57.7 degrees Celsius on Sept. 13, 1922 — the hottest ever measured. That would break most thermometers, which only go up to 50 on the Celsius scale!

THE FIRE TRIANGLE

Three elements are needed for a fire to start and then spread.

Fuel (to feed the flames)
Something that will burn, can be solid, liquid or gas.

Air (for it to breathe)
Fire needs oxygen and wind can provide it.

Heat (for it to continue to burn)
Dries out the fuel until it is dry enough to burn.

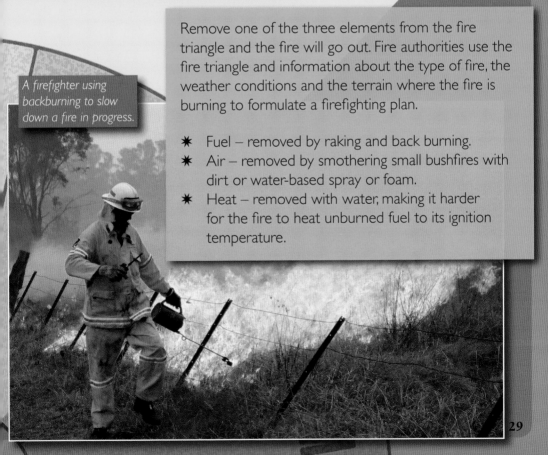

A firefighter using backburning to slow down a fire in progress.

Remove one of the three elements from the fire triangle and the fire will go out. Fire authorities use the fire triangle and information about the type of fire, the weather conditions and the terrain where the fire is burning to formulate a firefighting plan.

* Fuel – removed by raking and back burning.
* Air – removed by smothering small bushfires with dirt or water-based spray or foam.
* Heat – removed with water, making it harder for the fire to heat unburned fuel to its ignition temperature.

FIRE SPEED

Grass fires spread quickly – up to 20 km/h. There is much more fuel in a forest fire so they spread more slowly – usually less than 15 km/h. The more intense the fire, the greater the amount of hot air that is pushed ahead and the faster it spreads.

Fires tend to move two or three times faster when they are burning up steep, timbered slopes compared to flat ground. This is because the flames are closer to the ground as they travel up a slope.

Because hot air rises, smoke and gases rising from the fire quickly dry out these trees making them ignition ready. The air and wind can also carry sparks and embers up the slope and ignite spot fires.

Flames burn faster uphill.

FIRE & WIND

Head, Front
Spot Fire
Right Shoulder
The Black
Finger
Left Shoulder
Unburned Island
Left Flank
Right Flank
Origin
Green – the area outside the burn
Heel
Fire Perimeter – the line where the fire meets the unburned area

Wind provides oxygen to the fire and tilts the flames forward towards new fuel. As the fire spreads, its flames usually form a thin oval-shaped wall. The highest flames are at the front which is normally the most destructive part.

Lots of resources are available to do the job.

A change in wind direction can turn the long sides (flanks) of the fire into a wide fire front and dramatically increase the size of the fire. If the fire is large and the wind is strong, these conditions can create a fierce updraught of air called a convection column.

This column moves just ahead of the fire front and can fan flames to heights of up to 200 metres. Burning embers are sucked up by the convection column and are blown ahead by the wind.

Wind is a key ingredient in a fire. Without it, a fire would not be as large or as easily spread.

They can start spot fires several kilometres ahead of the fire front. This is generally how a fire can cross a road or a river.

massive convection column

31

Fire fighting machines

Who's Dennis?

The Dennis Sabre is now the Standard Fire Engine and is common at stations throughout the county. It is known as a Water Tender Ladder Rescue, as it holds water to extinguish a fire, ladders to help reach a fire and rescue equipment used for road traffic accidents. It also has other equipment like a Thermal Image Camera and Chemical Protection Suits. The gross weight of the vehicle is 13 tonnes!

Dennis fire engines are also used in Hong Kong.

Fighting fires from the air

A Boeing 747 has been turned into the 'World's biggest firefighter aircraft'. The 'Evergreen Supertanker' was made in California. Costing $50 million, it can dump 94,850 litres of water from 500 feet up. The aircraft can deal with wildfires and fight multiple fires in one flight. It can even fight fires at night.

A view from the air helps us know where we're needed.

DIDYOUKNOW?

The Tokyo fire department is the largest in the world, with 17,993 employees and a budget of US$2 billion (244 billion yen for fiscal year 2001.) Some 1,839 pieces of apparatus, including 20 firefighting motorcycles, are housed in 80 fire stations throughout Tokyo.

This helicopter has a water container to empty onto the flames.

The Aircranes can empty their entire tank!

Famous fires

World history is full of stories that blame great fires for the destruction of vast areas or entire cities. From the great fire that destroyed Rome in 64 B.C. to the fires that raged through the Australian landscape in 2002, fire remains one of man's most difficult battles.

The Great Chicago Fire

The Great Chicago fire is probably the most famous fire that occurred within the past two hundred years. This fire occurred on the evening of October 8, 1871. The summer of 1871 was unusually dry in Chicago. With all its wooden buildings, Chicago was kindling waiting to burn.

The fire killed 300 people and destroyed more than 17,000 structures in 27 hours. The origin of the fire is uncertain, though popular legend says Mrs. O'Leary was milking her cow at the start of the fire and it kicked over her lamp, setting the barn on fire and starting the spread of one of the biggest fires in history. The fire destroyed the entire downtown Chicago and most of its North side.

The Great Fire of London

This fire began in a baker's shop on September 2, 1666 and lasted for several days. At that time London was a city built largely of wood. Believe it or not, the Great London Fire had a reported death toll of only 6. It destroyed more than 13,000 buildings.

San Francisco Earthquake Fire

San Francisco's great fire occurred as a result of a tremendous earthquake that took place in the morning of April 18, 1906. Fires began from stoves and lamps that were overturned from the earthquake. The fire lasted for three days until firefighters decided to dynamite entire blocks to prevent the spread of the fire. This disaster killed 3,000 people and destroyed 300,000 buildings.

Hi, my name's Caroline, I work as a firefighter on Blue Watch at Gold Street Fire Station. I've been in the job for 9 months now and really love what I do.

ONE VERY HOT MONDAY

2.00 pm The Shout. On our way to our first incident of the day – a RTC (Road Traffic Collision) between a lorry and car. We had to release the driver, who was trapped in his car. It takes good teamwork between the police, ambulance crew and the Highways Agency to deal with this kind of situation.

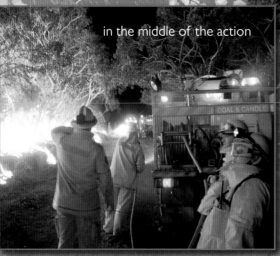

in the middle of the action

5.00 pm Back at the station we have a training session to test our procedures in dealing with a chemical leak. We all get involved and learn a lot – you really never stop learning in this job; even long-serving firefighters tell me that!

7.00 pm We're giving a talk to the local cubs group this evening. Part of our job is to make sure young people know about fire safety.

9.00 pm We get a shout to a large house fire. It's grown too big for the crew attending to deal with, so they've called for backup. My partner and I put on Breathing Apparatus (BA), grab a hose line and enter the house to check everyone is out. We tackle the fire and confine it to two rooms.

10:30 pm It feels like this day has gone on forever. I'm tired and filthy but the fire is now under control. No one has been hurt.

12:00 am Back at the station after a 10-hour day and we're exhausted. What a day!

The clean-up starts the next morning.

WHICH FIRE EXTINGUISHER?

There are different types of fire extinguishers. Be sure you know which types of extinguishers are designed for which fires. Remember: No single type of extinguisher is totally effective on every kind of fire.

- **Water** – for wood, paper and cloth fires only.
- **Dry chemical** – for live electrical equipment or flammable liquids and cooking oil.
- **Wet chemical** – for kitchen fires involving cooking oils or fat.
- **Foam** – for flammable or combustible liquids like petrol or paint. Can also be used for wood, paper and cloth fires.
- **Carbon dioxide** – used in laboratories or other areas which contain flammable liquids or sensitive electrical instruments.

There are also other powder and vaporising liquid extinguishers available for more specialised metal fires.

Keep your fire extinguishers handy.

FIRE EXTINGUISHER

firefighters testing extinguishers

FOAM
FIRE EXTIN
6 LITRE AFFF
1.3A
1 USE UPRIGHT

Extinguishers are clearly marked – read the instructions!

Know before you let go

Always check what extinguisher you have before using it. The wrong one could make the fire worse so know before you let go!

Top tips for home fire safety

1. Install and maintain working smoke alarms.

2. Create and practise your home escape plan.

3. Ensure your home security lets you out quickly. Keep keys in deadlocks.

4. Be safe in the kitchen. Do not leave cooking unattended and turn pot handles in.

5. Educate and supervise young children so they understand that fire is a tool not a toy. Keep matches and lighters out of reach.

6. Keep electrics away from water (leads and appliances).

7. Don't put anything metal in the microwave.

8. You are more at risk from a fire when asleep. So it's a good idea to check your home before you go to bed and shut all the doors.

Where's your nearest exit?

Is it working?

Holy smoke!

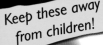

Keep these away from children!

A smoke alarm could save your life, giving you the valuable minutes you need to get out of the house. Follow these steps to have an effective smoke alarm system in your house.

1) Test your alarm once a month.

2) Change the batteries once a year or when the low battery signal beeps.

3) Replace smoke alarms every 10 years.

5) Fit an alarm in each bedroom of the house.

life saver

Follow these steps to become a firefighter

🔥 You must be at least 18 years old to become a firefighter. And remember, there is a lot of competition for jobs!

🔥 Each Fire Service sets its own entry requirements – you should contact the Chief Fire Officer (or recruitment officer) at the Fire Service you wish to join for details.

🔥 You will have physical, practical tests and an interview. There is no minimum or maximum height, but you must pass a test of fitness and strength.

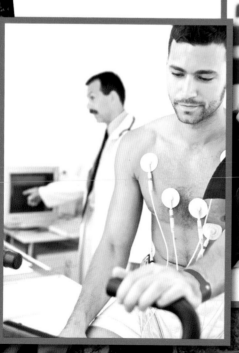

You must pass a medical exam as well as an eye test. This includes normal/ colour vision. No glasses or contact lenses are to be worn for this.

It is important that you have a good level of education as there are some brigades that may require some GCSEs. They may ask for certain grades and subjects. Some entrants already have A levels/AH or H grades or a degree.

If you are under eighteen years you can study BTEC Level three National Diploma in Public Services at a further education college. The idea of this course is to prepare for the pre-entry selection tests in order to become a firefighter. Contact your local college to find out if this course is available in your area.

CADET SCHEME

Some Fire & Rescue Services run Fire Cadet Units, giving young people aged 13 to 17 the opportunity to work with Fire & Rescue Service equipment and learn to work together as a team. They are shown how to use the equipment and also learn the technical information necessary.

Follow these steps to become a firefighter

Go there.....

www.fireservice.co.uk gives a wide range of advice on topics from filling in the application form correctly to how to pass the physical and mental tests. It also covers how to prepare for that all-important interview.

Basic training

The initial training takes 12 to 16 weeks. In Northern Ireland, it takes 18 weeks. In Scotland, you would attend a 16-week course at the Scottish Fire Training School. Following the initial training you will be posted at a Fire Station where you will become a Probationer for two years.
You will continue to learn by gaining experience and will be assessed continuously.

Keep on training . . .

Once qualified, Firefighters then work towards S/NVQ Level 2 and 3 in Emergency Fire Services. There are other work-based qualifications (S/NVQs) for the following roles: Crew Manager, Watch Manager, Station Manager, Group Manager and Area Manager will aid in future promotion opportunities.

Fire College

The Fire Service College is based in Moreton-In-Marsh in Gloucestershire. It provides specialist operational fire and rescue training in the UK for qualified firefighters. See page 45 for more details.

DIDYOUKNOW?

And finally...

You should remember that the Brigade is a uniformed disciplined service and respect for rank is expected of you. You have to wear a uniform at all times whilst you are on duty and to keep this clean and smart. There are rules you have to follow, for example, how to wear your hair.

43

OTHER RELATED AREAS

Other organisations who employ firefighters are:

- the British Airports Authority (BAA), which provides fire brigades at airports

- the Defence Fire and Rescue Service (DFRS), which provides fire services to military and other defence sites

- non-BAA airports and some large private organisations which have their own fire services

- the RAF

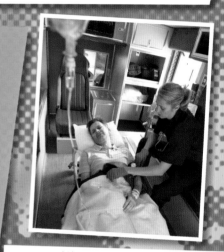

DIDYOUKNOW?

What to do if your clothes catch fire!

Don't run around, you'll make the flames worse. Lie down and roll around. It makes it harder for the fire to spread. Smother the flames with a heavy material, like a coat or blanket. **Remember, Stop, Drop and Roll!**

Within the emergency services, you might consider training as a police officer or ambulance paramedic; within the armed services, you could become an army serviceman/woman, RAF airman/woman, Royal Navy rating or an officer in the army, navy or air force. You could also think about becoming a Health and Safety Adviser or Police Community Support Officer.

Useful contacts

UK Fire Service Resources www.fireservice.co.uk

Fire Authority for Northern Ireland www.nifrs.org
Fire Authority for Northern Ireland, Human Resources,
Brigade Headquarters, 1 Seymour Street, Lisburn BT27 4SX.
Tel: 028 9266 4221

British Airports Authority (BAA) www.baa.com
Tel: 0141 585 6000

Communities and Local Government
www.communities.gov.uk/fire/working

Fire Gateway www.fire.gov.uk/careers

FRS Online www.frsonline.fire.gov.uk

Fire Service College www.fireservicecollege.ac.uk
Full details of courses available can be found on the website.

**Ministry of Defence (MoD) Defence Fire Training and
Development Centre** www.dftdc.org
Ministry of Defence (MoD) Defence Fire Training and Development
Centre, Manston, Ramsgate CT12 5BS. Tel: 01843 823351.

Just for fun:
Try out the Rapid Fire Game and test your skills at:
www.firekills.direct.gov.uk/index.html

Glossary

arson – the crime of deliberately starting a fire

back burning – intentionally setting fire to trees or bushes to create a gap so a bushfire can be stopped

DNA – deoxyribonucleic acid – found in the cells of all living things; passes on characteristics from parents to children; has a famous double helix structure

drill – routine practice of a procedure, e.g. fire drill

evacuations – when an area needs to be vacated due to danger, e.g. flood

fire resistant – able to keep out heat indefinitely

fire retardant – able to keep out heat for longer than normal

flash hood – soft cloth hood worn for more protection of the neck and face

hazardous materials – dangerous goods that must be handled with special equipment or clothing, e.g. acid

humidity – amount of moisture (water) in the air

ignite – to set on fire

logistics – the planning and carrying out of a complicated task

meteorology – scientific study of the weather

negligence – not giving proper care and attention

paramedic – person trained to give emergency first aid

radiation shield – protection from heat that radiates from a fire

roster – plan or list showing turns of duty

shout – an alarm at a fire station to tell firefighters they are needed

toxic – poisonous substance that can cause injury or death

trauma – deeply distressing experience, e.g. witnessing a death

visor – transparent moveable shield attached to a helmet to protect the eyes or face

Index

other titles in the series

PILOT

FORENSIC SCIENTIST

TV PRODUCER

MAGAZINE EDITOR

GAME DEVELOPER

MOTOR MECHANIC

ANIMATOR

BUILDER

CHEF

SPORTS TRAINER

FASHION DESIGNER

CHOREOGRAPHER

ZOO KEEPER

MARINE BIOLOGIST

LAWYER